Mr. Muddle's Little Green Book

A Guide For Hunting Lost Golf Balls

by

Harrison H. Farley MD

Haasf Publications
29615 Faith Court
Cannon Falls, MN 55009

Library of Congress Catalog Card Number 99-94068

Rules of a particular golf course, public or private, may preclude an individual from searching for lost golf balls.

ISBN # 0-9670461-0-6

Acknowledgment

I owe thanks to my daughter Julia Leahy for the original idea for the book; to my daughter Karen Lewis for the figure of Mr. Muddle and extensive critique of the text; to Jim Hjermstad for giving life to Mr. Muddle in his illustrations; to my wife Marie for help in virtually every aspect of the book; and lastly, to my brother G.M. Farley, the consummate ball hunter.
— H.H.F.

Table of Contents

Ball in the Woods

He walks the course
With mind adrift
No game today
His soul to lift.

He looks to find
A hidden ball
Covered by
The leaves that fall.

He cleans and stores it
Til next Spring,
Put back in play
A splendid thing.

Each small ball
Like a passing thought
Can serve a purpose
And should be sought.

Introduction

This small book describes the fine points of a pleasant exercise for the golfer who would like to replenish his supply of golf balls and at the same time lift his spirit. It's about saving and renewal, a reminder of times when things were repaired, not replaced.

I've tried to put one man's thoughts on a simple pastime in perspective. Should you elect to participate, you can walk and let off steam while picking up lost balls. You will be able to enjoy your course from a new point of view in a pressure-free environment. While tramping about, you'll be able to unwind and enjoy the natural beauty of the course without concern for "keeping the ball in play" or "hitting the fairways and greens."

Mr. Muddle has a way of looking at a golf course from a duffer's point of view. He never developed the knack of consistently hitting a ball well, though he spent a great deal of time practicing. It made him mad to keep losing balls. Out of pure frustration he developed an interest in searching for "the wayward ball." Surprisingly, it added a new dimension to the sport for him. Now with a healthy supply of balls at hand he could afford to lose a ball with impunity, and he had found a way of exercising that wasn't boring.

I met Mr. Muddle for the first time one early June evening when I was preparing to play the back nine holes of my golf course. I had seen the old guy on several occasions either hiking along the periphery of the course or prowling through the woods between the second and eighteenth fairways, carrying a bag in one hand and a golf club in the other. He had stopped at the water cooler on the 10th tee. After I had hit my tee-shot I walked over for a drink myself and was surprised to hear him compliment me on my drive. I thanked him and commented on the stash of balls he held in his hand. He smiled and said he had played his nine holes earlier in the day. He was presently out for the exercise and to pick up a few balls along the way.

"Looks as though you've found quite a few," I said.

The idea of an old guy traipsing about looking for balls was intriguing for I had always considered ball hunting to be a young man's activity. Our chat proved to be the beginning of a friendship that developed over the course of the summer and it led eventually to my writing this short book about his favorite pastime.

If you are at a point in your life where you feel the need for a diversionary activity with a positive endpoint and a chance to get away from it all while meditating on the "big picture," then a walk around the golf course hunting balls could be just the thing for you. The discovery of a fine golf ball hidden in the grass or leaves is a pleasant experience. Follow the tips Mr. Muddle provides and put in your time (instead of the drudgery of a treadmill) and you will find a lot of balls **and** improve your health.

Portrait of the Ball Hunter

What kind of man would walk around a golf course looking for golf balls? Someone dense between the ears? An old skinflint? So it seemed to me before I met Mr. Muddle.

It was a surprise to learn that Malcomb Muddle was a retired surgeon. Somehow he didn't look the part. I quickly addressed him as "Doctor" but he set me straight. "You can save that moniker for the docs who are still practicing, Bud," he said, "And don't call me Malcomb either!" It was Mr. Muddle or just plain Muddle from that point on.

He had practiced general surgery for thirty years in Minneapolis. His life had been one consumed by work and family. After he had seen the last patient of the day he would head for home. During the frantic drive on the freeway he underwent a metamorphosis to become father and spouse in his busy household. There was little time for other activity in his life. Hunting golf balls certainly never entered his mind.

This all changed the moment he walked out of his office for the last time. It was as if he had been sucked up by a tornado, whirled about, and returned to earth. His priorities changed and he saw himself in a different light. No longer the indestructible physician, he realized his life was finite, and the clock was ticking. After much discussion with his wife, they reached a mutual decision. They would leave the bustle of the metropolis and move to a more peaceful environment. They found a pleasant rural community southeast of Minneapolis that seemed just right for them and moved on. It made for a big change in their lifestyle.

It dawned on Muddle that the advice he'd given patients should apply to himself. He needed to exercise more. He needed to lose weight and he had to work on lowering his blood pressure. He was spending too much time in his overstuffed chair (a mystery book on his lap!) with his head back contemplating "the big picture." It was pleasurable but it came with a price. His pants no longer fit and his general physical condition was deteriorating. To burn off calories and combat this slide into a sedentary existence he renewed an old interest in the game of golf.

A fine public golf course was no more than five minutes by car from his home. I can attest to its wealth of natural topographical variety. It was designed to blend into the lay of the land. There were (and are) hills and valleys, forests and thickets and a continual source of water from natural springs. Hazards came with the territory! It was both interesting and challenging and the price was right! The course was a veritable gem!

Muddle found out to his dismay that he wasn't much of a golfer. It was painfully obvious that it would take much work if he were to improve. He did practice mightily but he found it hard to change his flawed swing. Still, what joy it was to be on his course, to smell the new mown grass and hear the distinctive click of a well-struck ball-when it happened! His consolation-even on a bad day, being on the golf course beat walking his treadmill!

Yet, two or three rounds a week was insufficient exercise. His brother (GMF), an inveterate golf ball hunter, had for years touted the benefits of searching for lost balls. Muddle decided to try it himself. He would walk the woods and hills of his course for relaxation and exercise when he wasn't playing and in the process recover a few of the balls he had lost.

He felt better after his very first walk. It was a pleasant surprise to find an activity that was so rewarding! Muddle was ready for more. He decided that whenever he felt the need to exercise, and didn't wish to play, he'd take a brisk walk through the high grass and woods and search for lost balls. The exercise should be invigorating and, hopefully, he'd collect some balls to show for his effort.

It didn't take long to discover that on certain days he'd find quite a few but on other days he'd be less successful. It dawned on him that he should study the course and keep in mind where and when his outings had been successful. What began as a novelty had become a *passion!*

During the next few months after our meeting at the watercooler he let me in on the secret to his success. He described and analyzed the manner in which players lose balls and where they're likely to be found. He felt that these tips could be applied to other courses and would help a novice ball hunter.

Should you wish to take up this activity, here are three caveats that Muddle makes. First, be a member of the course where you hunt (don't expect any kudos from your course manager)! Second, don't waste your time on newly constructed courses that are surrounded by homes and landscaped yards. They have few natural hazards like woods, high grass and thickets and although they may be delightful to play, the only balls lost are those that end up in ponds beyond the reach of the golfer standing on the bank. Third, poisonous snakes in western desert courses and alligators in the mangrove marshes of the deep south constitute a real threat. It doesn't make sense to risk "life and limb" where the roughs and hazards are dangerous. Ball hunt with caution on such a course.

Muddle and his brother (GMF) learned the joy of searching for lost balls on their local public golf course when they were boys. The monetary value of a golf ball was relatively greater fifty years ago than it is today. However, the value of the ball paled in importance to the act of discovery. There's a certain unique smell to the mown grass of the fairways and greens and a satisfying beauty in the layout of a course that leaves a lasting impression on a boy (or girl!). The boys got hooked by the mystique of the game!

A non-golfer watching a match on television might wonder if there are enough balls lost during play to justify this kind of activity, for professionals seldom lose a ball during a round. Not so Muddle and his buddies! They are light years apart from those guys! He told me that an observer watching his group tee-off would understand why so many balls disappear. They come flying off the tee in all directions. They are sliced, hooked, dribbled and sent rocketing into the most unlikely of places!

Losing track of the ball

Muddle analyzed his own failings. He lost a lot of balls-and it was no wonder. He had the bad habit of staring interminably at a good hit (how many straight hits are lost?) but when he hit a "flyer" he would turn away in disgust. He would be better served to reverse the reactions. A "flyer" should be followed closely by lining it up with a distant tree or marker. A quick glance isn't good enough when a ball is hit into the type of rough on our course. He would usually make an obligatory search but if the ball landed in high grass, a thicket, or a marsh, he wouldn't find it. He'd quickly take out a spare that he keeps handy, take a drop and a penalty stroke and ignore the lost ball rule!

Brown Study

Mr. Muddle maintains that over time the bottom line of his pastime has changed. From ball recovery it is now an opportunity to dump stress and enjoy a place of tranquillity; in a word, be recharged. He likes to walk and think, to test ideas, but also to simply let his mind drift in limbo. There is no deadline to meet in the woods, no thought of winning or losing. It's a place apart in time and space and conducive to positive thinking. He spends a good deal of time counting his blessings and he feels revitalized when he arrives at home.

Getting Ready to Hunt

Attitude

To be successful hunting balls you must have the right attitude. Compare it with looking for agates on the north shore of Lake Superior or for shark's teeth on the gulf beaches of west Florida. Some people never find what they are looking for *because of low expectations.* A ball hunter can enjoy nature and allow his mind to roam at the same time but when he approaches certain thickets or areas of the woods where he has previously had success he should flip on his *awareness* switch.

"It makes a difference, Bud (that's what he calls me)! Put yourself in a *positive* frame of mind."

Attire

Comfort and function are the watchwords in clothing to wear while hunting balls. There is no reason for concern about the latest clubhouse dress code when you plan to look for balls.

"I was refused the right to play by a little clubhouse snippet because I was wearing a pair of jeans (expensive ones too)," Muddle said. "There's no rule enforcer like that out in the woods."

I reminded him that there were good reasons for some of the seemingly haughty club golf rules.

"Have it your own way!" he replied.

Old clothes are fine but one needs to use good judgment. It's a good idea to protect your arms and legs. Although short pants and short sleeves are comfortable they leave your limbs unnecessarily exposed.

"Don't be concerned with style, Bud; you're unlikely to meet someone in the woods you'll need to impress."

Mosquitoes and gnats are a problem in the woods and in the tall grass. You can minimize the number of bites you'll get by using a repellent on your wrists and the nape of your neck. These little pests, along with ticks and flies, abound at various times during the summer months. They're most prevalent at dusk.

It is important to use proper footwear. The best shoe allows for traction, and protection against cold and dampness. During the summer months, an old pair of golf shoes with steel spikes works the best. Spikes are particularly helpful on steep slopes like those on hole #2 or #8. Don't try to negotiate hills wearing slick soled shoes or you'll find yourself nursing a bruised hip-or worse! On the other hand, if your plan is to enter a marsh you'll need to wear a waterproof shoe. It's an excellent place to hunt because golfers seldom venture in after a stray ball. The chance of a golfer finding a ball hit into either the marsh on #3 or #7 is slim at best for no one wants to risk having to play the rest of a round with soaked feet.

Cold weather curtails golf in the fall but not ball hunting. It is a marvelous season to search because play is either at a minimum or it has been suspended altogether. Many of Muddle's cronies depart for warmer pasture and he has the course practically to himself. Poor circulation requires that he pay particular attention to keeping his hands and feet warm. He favors wearing a pair of waterproof hunting boots and he takes along an extra pair of gloves in cold weather. Balls picked from ponds and marshes are wet. As he removes them from the suction cup on the iron or from his retriever, he finds it doesn't take long to soak through a pair of gloves. It's a real pleasure to slide his hands into a dry pair for the walk home.

"What color of clothes should one wear, Mr. Muddle?" I ask.

"No need to make a fashion statement."

If you hunt in the woods while others play, you'll want to be as unobtrusive as possible. This doesn't mean you need a camouflage outfit but leave the bright shirt you bought in Hawaii at home. Earth colored clothing works the best.

Cover your head. Insect bites on the scalp can be unpleasant. And protect your eyes. Walking through the woods while looking at the ground for balls is a good way to get stuck with a sharp branch so the ball hawk must be careful. All these things are important but above all, be comfortable.

Equipment

Muddle says that there are only two crucial items to take on a walk—some type of retriever and a bag for carrying balls. Better yet two bags, one plastic bag placed inside another will serve a double function. It lends added strength when needed for a heavy load or it can be used separately on a really big day. Mr. Muddle's brother has on occasion, filled one bag, ditched it and filled another. The following day while playing a round, a brief foray into the woods and out he comes with a full bag of balls!

An old iron with a rubber suction cup attached to the handle end provides a serviceable tool to carry, or you can buy a retractable trap device at practically any general store. These extendible retrievers are usually 10 feet long. A word to the wise! Balls seen in the water are frequently just out of reach of the standard retriever—but fourteen footers are also sold! Think about it if you intend to buy a retriever!

If you want to concentrate on marshes, creeks, and standing water, the extendible retriever is the tool to carry. If your intent is to search the woods and thickets, and particularly the hillsides, then it is better to carry an iron with attached cup for picking up balls. An iron is also sturdy enough to prevent a tumble when you hunt on a hillside like the ravine on Hole #8. Either of the tools can and should be used rather than a bare hand to extract a ball from a patch of suspicious green vegetation. It is easy to get excited and rush to pick up an excellent ball lying right in the middle of a patch of poison ivy!

If a ball is seen in the water close to shore it can be recovered with the help of the iron but it requires a skillful touch. With practice a hawk can land a ball balanced on the blade of the iron by delicately moving it through the water. The cup will usually fail to grip a ball under water, especially when the bottom is soft and there's no resistance.

'Easy does it!'

Lastly, in a worst case scenario, use the club to ward off snakes or other critters!

Tips to Finding Balls

Analyze the Course

Mr. Muddle has carefully analyzed our course from the standpoint of finding lost balls. This is quite different from studying the course to improve his score. It would be more appropriate to say "how not to play the course." Muddle made more than his share of wild shots as he resumed playing golf after his long layoff. During the search for his own errant balls quite often he ran into others and he soon realized that there were specific areas of high probability. He made a mental note of where these balls seemed to accumulate.

"I'll tell you, Bud," he said. "If someone wants to be successful at ball hunting, the first thing he must do is to analyze his course."

Our eighteen hole layout is bordered by the Cannon River. It is ideal for ordinary day to day play. It was constructed with the intent to keep things as natural as possible-just the opposite of a modern, manicured high-profile course. The creeks and hills, oaks and thickets were left in place when it was constructed. If a golfer keeps his ball in the fairway he'll score well, but if he is prone to hit stray shots his score will soar and he'll need plenty of spare balls. As a golfer Muddle found the course demanding, but as a ball hunter it was and is very rewarding.

The woods are dense; there are areas of very tall grass and there is an abundance of water. Streams cross the fairways; marshes gobble up stray balls, lakes must be over-flown and the river roars alongside two of the holes. Is it any wonder that balls disappear!

Study the topography of the six holes illustrated in the appendix. Muddle makes the point that the chance of losing a ball increases markedly when you lose sight of it during its flight. Look at the woods, the areas of tall grass, and the thickets. A ball hit into or through these hazards becomes invisible. Note that spring water seeps from the hills to form streams and marshes, and eventually lakes. Water is certainly one of the key natural hazards on this course. Lilies, underwater vegetation, and surface plant growth all tend to hide balls. Six times on the back nine the golfer must hit over water. The water meanders toward the river which ribbons two holes of the course. Lost balls, waiting to be discovered, lay partially or completely hidden by silt in the bed of the streams all along the way.

There are a few holes where a wayward drive will land in an adjacent fairway and remain in play; but of the four major distance errors-right, left, short or long-one, two or three come into play on most tees. Poorly hit balls are easily lost. The big hitter who has a difficult time keeping his drives in the fairway will be in constant trouble.

Dub or dribble a hit into tall grass close to the tee and it often will be found, but if it is hit 200+ yards into tall grass it will disappear because the golfer won't be able to get a good read on it. This is most apparent on Hole #1 with the trees just to the right of the elevated tee. The cluster of big oaks is not only a barrier to ball flight but it obstructs the golfer's vision from what lies beyond. A ball lined directly into these trees will frequently remain in play because the grass underneath is sparse and short. On the other hand, the big hit, if it goes over the trees or slices around them, will pose a major problem, for it will land in the tall thick grass. During the summer a golfer will spend little time searching for his ball in there. Ticks and pesky mosquitoes lurk in the tall grass. Nevertheless this long grassy slope, for reasons referred to later, is one of the best areas to find excellent balls.

Hole #2. Slice or hook the ball off this elevated tee and you're in trouble. Note the woodsy hills on either side. They are tough to negotiate. Briars add to the poor soul's problem who searches there for his wayward ball. And pity the golfer who should wear short sleeves and short pants when he ventures into these woods. He will be so busy slapping at insects that he'll make but a cursory search. Safe to say, golf balls accumulate here.

Study the diagram of Hole #8. It is situated on a flat plane 100 feet above the major water hole (Hole #13). If a golfer has driven correctly from the tee he can follow the edge of the ravine and enjoy the marvelous scenery below as he walks to his ball, but he's out of luck if his ball goes into the ravine. The grassy hill leading downward is steep and the loose sandy soil is treacherous to negotiate. The fairway bends gently around it. Any ball hit over the edge (and there are many) is gone. A serious golfer will never take the time to search down that hill for an errant ball while playing a round. Down at the bottom it sometimes looks like a field of dandelions going to seed!

Hole #4 is a nightmare for a golfer who tends to slice the ball. Although it is a short par five, for the first 220 yards a row of trees and briars 10 yards wide separates the narrow fairway from the river. Balls hit to the right here often end up in the river! Let's assume your ball does not reach the river but is found unplayable in the woods beyond the red stakes. After you take a drop your second hit must not slice or, it too, will find trouble in the woods or tall grass. Are you getting the picture? Many balls are lost on this hole.

Ball Distribution

Muddle told me that in order for a ball hunter to make the most of his time he must determine the spots likely to garner the largest number of *retrievable* balls. Hole #13 with its surrounding lake would seem to head that list, but any ball hit into the shallow water around the green and within ten feet of shore can readily be recovered by the golfer who has hit the errant shot. If he doesn't have a retriever in his bag, the next guy along who is better prepared will snare it. It follows that even though many balls end up in the water on this hole, the knowledgeable ball hawk will spend little time here (note discussion of seasonal change).

"Ask yourself this question, Bud," Muddle said. "Where would you look if you wanted to find balls in the best condition?"

That was a tough one.

"Think about the big hitter, how he likes to use the newest, most expensive, and latest ball to be advertised. Now look again at Hole #1. The area of tall grass well out beyond the oak trees will contain many balls, and usually they will be of the highest quality. It is the *first* hole, and most golfers at least like to start a round with a high quality ball. That area is easily reached by the big hitter. The golfer teeing up on #1 surveys the scene ahead and doesn't expect to lose a ball. He can't see what is behind the clump of trees on his right. In the back of his mind he may remember that tall grass, but on his first crucial swing (often with an audience!) he is thinking mainly of making good contact and avoiding the trees. Well, if he should push it over the trees or slice it around the trees, it's lost in the grass.

"Vis-a-vis #7. The rough on both sides of the narrow fairway consists of marsh akin to quicksand. Though it is laden with lost balls, many are of poor quality. The golfer preparing to tee-off gazes at the green two hundred yards away and says to himself, 'I might lose one here!' He fishes about in his pocket for a 'less than best' ball. If you were to put on a pair of 'waders' and venture out amongst the tall reeds to the right of the fairway or the thick grass growing in the marsh to the left of the fairway, you would indeed recover many balls. However, there would be a high percentage of 'cheapies,' oldies, X-outs, yellows, pinks, and blues. The lesson is obvious: leave the balls lost here for someone else."

The old guy had put a great deal of thought into this business. One evening during the summer I went out to try my hand at hunting balls. There were only a few golfers left on the course, but when I arrived at #7 a twosome was preparing to hit. I spotted Muddle kibitzing with the golfers from a bench behind the blue tees. When one of the golfers sliced a long iron shot into the thicket to the right of the green, Mr. Muddle reached into his bag of balls and rolled one out to the golfer— a gift "Mulligan." The golfer smiled and tee'd it up. Again it sailed far out to the right. Muddle rolled out two more before the golfer could put one on the green. After the twosome had started down the fairway I came up and sat down by the old geezer. He had obviously enjoyed his little repartee with the young men. Beside him on the bench was a bag full of balls.

"That kid can really hit a ball, Bud, but I think he's blocking a bit on his swing. Say, where's your retriever?" he asked.

I told him that I had forgotten it. I hated to admit to having just a half dozen balls in my pocket with his full bag sitting beside me. He shook his head in disgust.

"Some guys are slow learners," he said.

He was trying to balance a ball on the blade of an old iron. I knew that wasn't an easy thing to do. He winked at me. "Care to try it?" he asked.

I tried but was not successful.

"My brother learned this trick from his son. He maintains they can retrieve any ball in the water within reach of an iron!"

This led to a conversation on several little-known places where balls can accumulate.

"There are a lot of subtleties in this business that you'll need to learn, Bud," he said.

He described how a ball dribbled close by an elevated tee may run down a steep slope into weeds or a thicket. It is gone and quickly forgotten although in reality it lies only a few yards away.

"I'd go after it," I said.

Muddle laughed.

"No you wouldn't, you'd be too embarrassed! The guy that hit a shot like that wouldn't be ready to negotiate that type of hill during play. He'd want the pitiful hit out of his mind. He would probably hit another and act as if he'd never before blown such a tee shot! Yet the ball is close at hand.

It is a great place to check when you're ball hunting but you have to plan ahead. Shoes that allow for good traction are a must and you definitely need a retriever to reach the ball if it rests in a perilous spot! It will also take some delicate footwork and a little effort but you'll find some good balls there."

It was getting dark but he had more to say.

"Have you ever looked *behind* a tee, Bud?" he asked.

"No-seems like that would be a waste of time."

He told me then how in the early spring after the snow had melted, he had stood on the fifth tee thinking about nothing in particular when he happened to see a fine ball in the grass behind and to the side of the tee mound. The area had been covered with tall thick grass but the packed snow had beaten it down, and with a thaw the ball became visible. He picked it up—then he saw another, and another! How did those balls get there?

Muddle's analysis—The fifth and sixth holes lie side by side but reversed

180 degrees in direction. The golfer hitting down the sixth fairway must look directly into the sun in the afternoon. In the summer when the ground is dry a ball gets a lot of roll if it is hooked or hit left on the approach shot to the *sixth* green, and it can find its way over to and across the *fifth* tee. There it comes to rest in the tall grass. The golfer is unsure of its exact location. When he sheepishly approaches the fifth tee to look around, another group of players arrives to tee-off. The golfer chasing the errant ball is so embarrassed by his poor shot that all he wants is to get out of the way. He makes a perfunctory search, then drops a ball and plays out the hole (thus ignoring rule 27-1!). The ball he has hit across the fifth tee remains in the tall grass and is forgotten.

Macho Factor

"Seems like a golfer's psyche gets him in trouble," I said.

"His ego interferes with his *judgment* and it makes for balls ending up in some unlikely spots. I've found them close to or behind the white tees on certain holes. Seems like it's a *guy* thing! A man might feel pushed to make the big hit, or he might have hit one or two long drives and decide it was time for him to play with the 'big boys.' In either case, he moves to the blue tees (or those well behind the average golfer's tee) even though he doesn't belong there. Now he's under tremendous pressure to hit his best drive. This leads to a fair number of miss-hits. The miss-hit drive can dribble anywhere and many times the golfer himself is too ashamed to go looking for it. It may not have even passed the *white* tee. Any rough adjacent to the tee box should be checked for balls."

I'd had enough-the old guy had struck a nerve! But he had more to say.

Bonanza Days

"Watch the bulletin board in the clubhouse for scheduled special event days. Hunting is often very good following one of these match/parties (I knew about them for I'd been locked out from playing a number of times because of such an event).

Local business or service organizations sponsor them as an employee morale booster. The sponsor often includes a sleeve of new balls. It's the only golf outing of the year for many of the 'boys.' They're out for a good time and they won't spend much time chasing down stray hits. Keep alert for such an event!"

Effect of Change in Climate

By the time September arrived I thought that I had just about exhausted Mr. Muddle's thoughts on ball hunting. His tips were helping me to fill the bag I now carried during my walks.

I ran into him on Hole #4. He was standing on the elevated riverbank gazing down at the fast moving water below. I asked if he was depressed about soon having to give up his hobby for the winter. I got an earful!

"Let me tell you how ball hunting changes in the fall and winter, Bud," he said.

A change in the weather and/or season affects where you find balls and your ability to get to them. He told me that a farmer's field lies alongside a fairway on his brother's golf course. During the growing season, balls hit into the corn or beans are off limits. But immediately following the crop harvest, the balls lie exposed and he has a real "field day!"

At any time during the golfing season, a prolonged dry spell can produce a significant change in the water level in the ponds. Balls previously hidden from view become obvious. Even the Cannon River bottom is accessible at times.

He chuckled, then related how he and a friend had stood looking down at the river during a hot spell in July, much as we were presently doing, when to their surprise two teenage boys floated into view on inner tubes. As the boys passed over balls in the shallow water they snatched them up howling with glee. For temporary storage they threw them on patches of exposed river bottom. Then they worked their way upstream and repeated the process. Muddle said that he shook his fist at them in mock anger but the boys only laughed. They couldn't care less! They were safe in the river!

Cannon River 'Gold Mine'

"In the fall," he said, "a lot of changes take place and I really get fired up about ball hunting. It's a prime time to hunt with no ticks or mosquitoes and just a few hard-core golfers still playing. The ground cover changes radically; grass withers away. Leaves are a problem when they first fall from thc trccs, but a good rain or snow causcs thcm to dcteriorate and those telltale white spots begin to appear!

"The 'Snowbirds' fly west and south and most golfers hang it up for the year, but not this guy!"

In the fall when insects have disappeared and there is better visibility (no leaves), Muddle can reach the center of bordering thickets that were inaccessible during the summer months. Balls have been washed along in the streams and come to rest behind logs or in deep eddy pools in these thickets well away from the fairways. The inveterate ball hawk in late

October and November can harvest a trove of lost balls there with a little effort. They collect two, three, four at a time. They may have a light coating of sediment but they're easily cleansed and can be restored to a pristine condition.

'Top Secret'

Muddle discovered purely by good fortune another little known reason for hunting balls late in the year. Few are aware of it. It has to do with *ball movement.* Like rocks in a farmer's soil, balls buried in the marshes, streams and ponds will be forced upward and outward with a hard freeze. Balls completely hidden from view become visible. He maintains that this astounding occurrence must be experienced to be believed. Shallow water next to an embankment (Hole #13) will be void of balls one day and contain many a few days later! They are forced out of the soft bank and roll down to the bottom. If there is no overlying ice, they can be retrieved.

Winter-then Spring

Eventually when the ground is frozen solid and snow blankets the golf course Mr. Muddle calls it quits. His spirit sags and like an overstuffed bear (literally), he goes into hibernation. He finds it hard to bear the long down-time during the winter months and occasionally he'll put on his warm boots and walk the course for exercise.

"Even with snow covering the ground I've walked the course and seen some wondrous sights. The river keeps flowing throughout the winter and the rapids along Hole #4 are mostly ice free. Twice I've stood right here and looked down upon an Asian family fishing with light line and floating lures."

"Fishing from shore?"

"No. They have amazing perseverance. With the water level low they were able to get out on an island of rocks where they could easily flip their lures into the channels of fast moving water. They even had a little fire going to keep warm and they had a bucketful of fish!"

Spots for Rest and Contemplation

During one of our last chats Muddle said that hunting for balls while walking the course provides him a pleasant opportunity for thoughtful reflection and appreciation of his blessings. Life just looks better when viewed from a bridge spanning a stream of fresh spring water or kicking through the leaves in a forest of oaks.

"Do you remember Al Capp, Bud?"

Yes, I remembered the famous cartoonist who created "Lil Abner."

"Capp joked about 'a man letting his mind go slack.' That's what I do while walking the course. It's not a way to do your best while playing a round, of course. It's best to concentrate on your game. Still, there's always the 'exception that proves the rule.' Once, a golfer in my threesome, while waiting impatiently on a slow group ahead of us, took a light fishing rod from his cart and cast an artificial worm into the stream that crossed the fairway."

Muddle couldn't hide a smile.

"He had time to catch two nice bass (and release them) before continuing on to par the hole!"

That was a fine story!

"Better not try it, Bud," he said, laughing. "I don't recommend it!"

The sight and sound of spring water trickling out of a hillside is invigorating to one's thought processes. The spring water coalesces into streams and eventually forms a lake around hole #13. This is fine habitat for fish and turtles and a variety of birds. The water moves slowly on to the Cannon River. At the same delightful spot on the river where the fishing is good an eagle will occasionally swoop down for a meal.

"You can get a great deal more from this course than just golf!" he said.

"Do you like poetry, Bud?"

"Not especially," I replied truthfully.

He ignored my negative response and recited a poem he wrote called "Ball in the Woods."

"What do you think?" he asked hopefully.

"Not bad-not bad, Mr. Muddle."

I didn't want to hurt his feelings, but it sounded more like an old Burma Shave ad than a Shakespearean sonnet.

Bird houses, strategically placed around the course, bustle with activity during the nesting season. Red winged blackbirds hover in the thicket alongside the tee of Hole #13. Bluebirds and purple martins are commonly seen around the houses set up by the maintenance crew. Canadian Geese sometimes cluster in such numbers on Hole #13 that they are actually a nuisance for golfers and greenskeepers alike.

"Generation X would do well to emulate these birds," he said. "They keep close watch over their goslings."

Standing close by the green on Hole #9 are two apple trees. In September these trees produce a large number of juicy and tasty treats. Late in the month I saw him sitting on a nearby bench, apple in hand. It was one of those magnificent fall afternoons in Minnesota. I went over and sat down beside him and I must have had an accusatory look on my face.

Brown Study

"It's OK, Bud," he reassured me. "They're free; nobody minds. You'd better try one."

He told me that one of the women golfers claimed they made excellent apple pies! Muddle looked up at me and said thoughtfully,

"There's so much out here that people miss while playing a round because everyone has to keep moving. There is no time to loiter. Not so while ball hunting, you can spend time with your thoughts. And best of all Bud, for me it's similar to the healing arts, it's about salvage and reclamation."

He seemed rather distant, staring down the fairway. I think his thoughts were far from golf. I didn't want to intrude any longer so I slipped off to make the most out of what remained of the day.

Grading Balls

Mr. Muddle does not sell used golf balls, he gives them away. Nevertheless, he does consider their value. Used balls may be purchased rather cheaply in stores or by mail order, sight unseen. They are offered for sale in every type of retail outlet from service stations to pro shops. These balls differ in value and there is absolutely no way of knowing prior to purchase the true condition of the ball. A ball may be severely damaged by exposure to the extremes of temperature and still look fine. There is nothing more discouraging to a golfer than to hit a good drive which should have gone 250 yards, peter out at 150! How can a golfer about to purchase a used ball judge its condition and thus its worth? He can't! Although the make and type of ball is of some help, still, they are difficult to evaluate. They should be tested.

All golf balls deteriorate with time. It is said that the shelf life of a golf ball varies from 2-5 years. Thus, one clue to value is the name (for original cost) and information stamped on the ball. If the purchaser knows it was made over five years ago it will have undergone some deterioration no matter how good it looks.

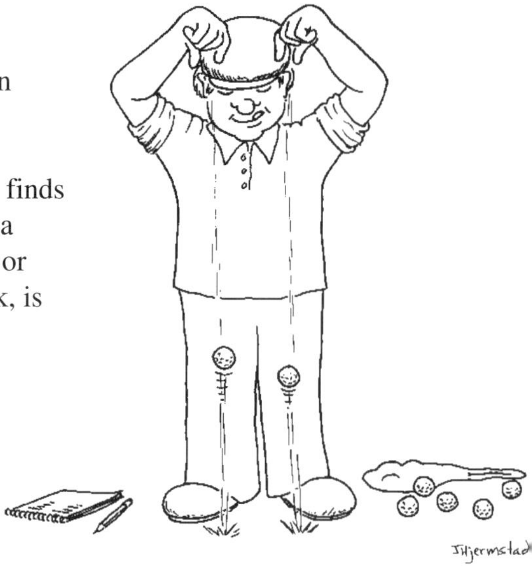

Mr. Muddle puts the balls he finds into his utility room sink for a quick wash-up. A 'cheapie,' or ball with a serious scuff mark, is placed into a practice-ball container. He grades the remaining balls on two criteria. First, the outward appearance 1-4. Second, the critical *bouncibility factor.*

To determine this factor he uses the best new two piece bouncer in his bag as a standard and compares the recovered ball to it. He assigns a 1-10 rating by 'guesstimation.' (Muddle is working with an inventor buddy of his to develop a practical and simple device that will enable him to more accurately rate this factor).

He then calculates the value of the used ball by multiplying the exterior grade times the bouncibility factor and arrives at a value quotient (V.Q.). The number is relative, but it helps! The best possible rating for a used ball by this methodology is 40.

A ball with a V.Q. of 36-40 is virtually as good as new. If the ball has a soft cover, produced for maximum spin, it will have less rebound at six feet than the usual two-piece ball. It must be compared against a test ball of similar construction. It is more difficult to judge and Muddle to date has not been satisfied with his rating of this type of ball. However, his is a work in progress. It does seem certain that a rating system would be helpful in determining the proper price for a used golf ball in the market-place.

Postscript

On an unseasonably warm November day (just before I left for Florida!) I went down to the course for a nice walk only to find Mr. Muddle preparing to play a round of golf. The course was closed to all but members and no one was allowed on the greens. The cups and flags were placed about twenty yards short of the regular greens. It was our last occasion to talk for some time and I asked him if he would mind if I wrote a small book on his favorite pastime, with some of the thoughts he had passed along to me during our "talks." He told me it was fine with him but that he thought it was kind of crazy to think that people would be interested in reading about such a mundane subject.

"I don't know-I think it has a lot of merit," I said.

"Suit yourself, Bud. You know, maybe it is the sort of relaxation we need in these fast times. I know that I can't begin to keep up with all the changes taking place. It boggles the mind. Is there a place more conducive to productive thought than right here in this beautiful setting?"

He answered his own question, "Well, maybe in Church or Synagogue."

"This is a great place to meditate. When I'm out here surrounded by nature - the future looks hopeful. I think positive thoughts. Climbing the hills, ducking under shrubs and stretching for balls, every now and again I'll pick up a discarded beer can and throw it in my bag to trash it in the next available receptacle. That's what all of us should be doing all the time-keeping the world decent for those who follow us.

"Ball hunting can be a good place to restore emotional tranquility-a *brown study*, if you will. It is good for you mentally and physically. You should make it a habit. Put your clubs down every now and then and give your game a rest. Listen to the birds. Enjoy the wildflowers. Stop on one of the bridges and watch the fish below and put your life in order. Best of all-you'll never have to worry about running short of golfballs again!"

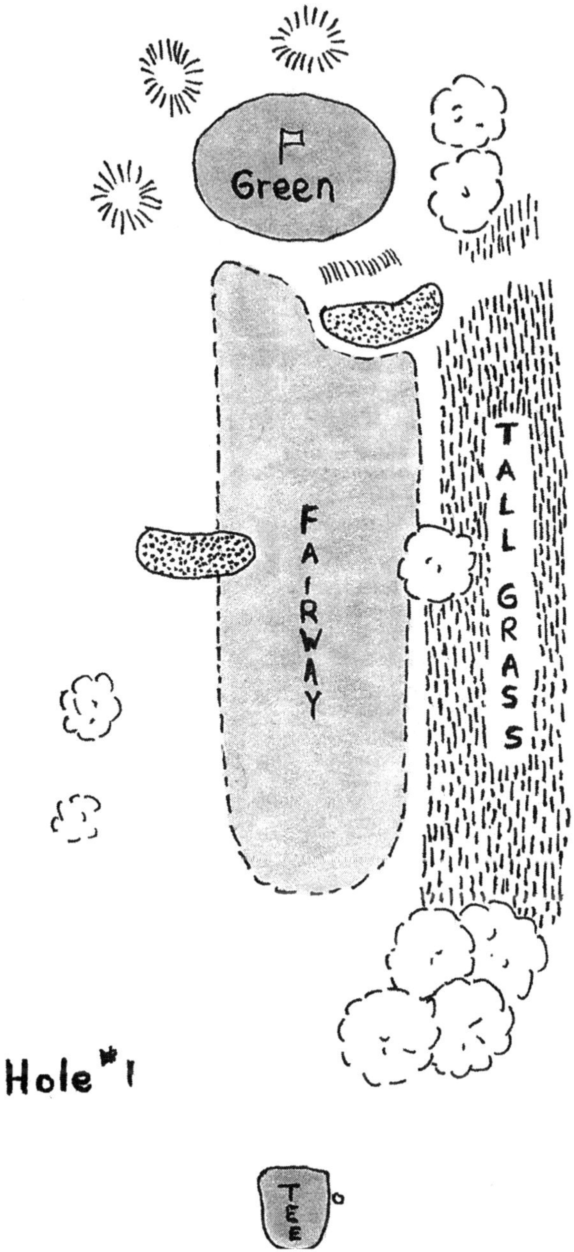
Green
FAIRWAY
TALL GRASS
Hole #1
TEE

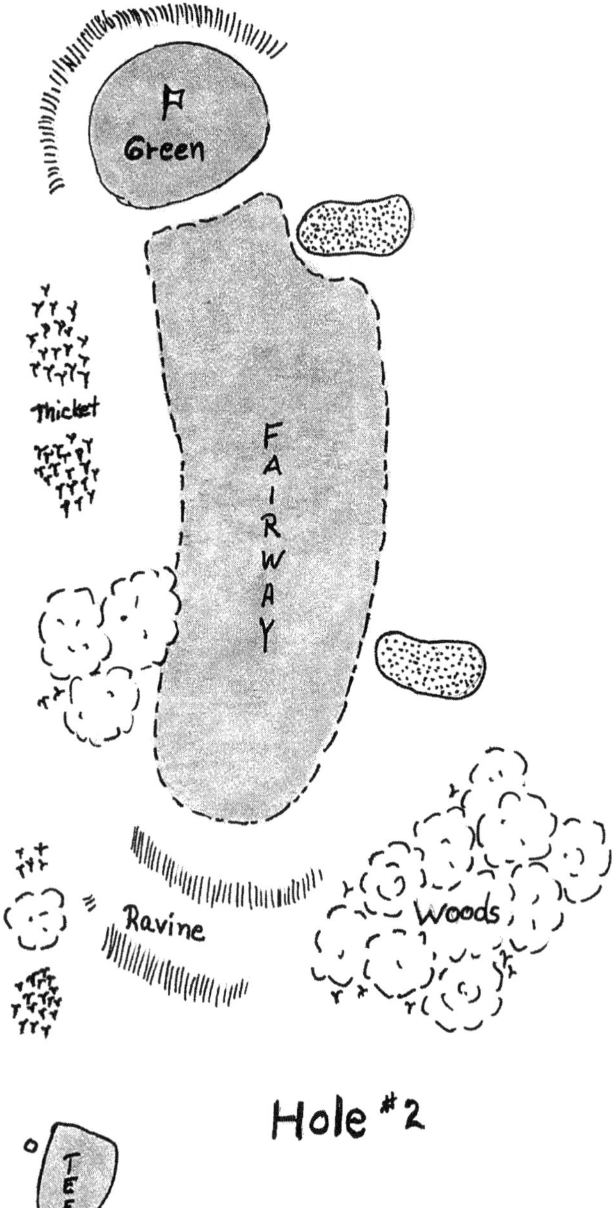
Green
Thicket
FAIRWAY
Ravine
Woods
Hole #2
TEE

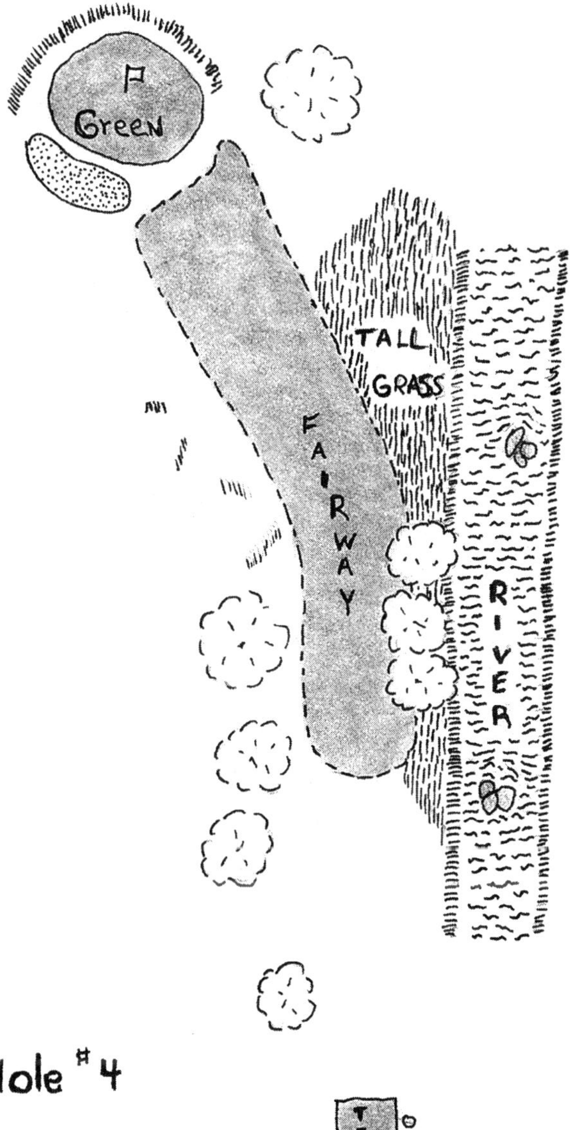

Hole # 4

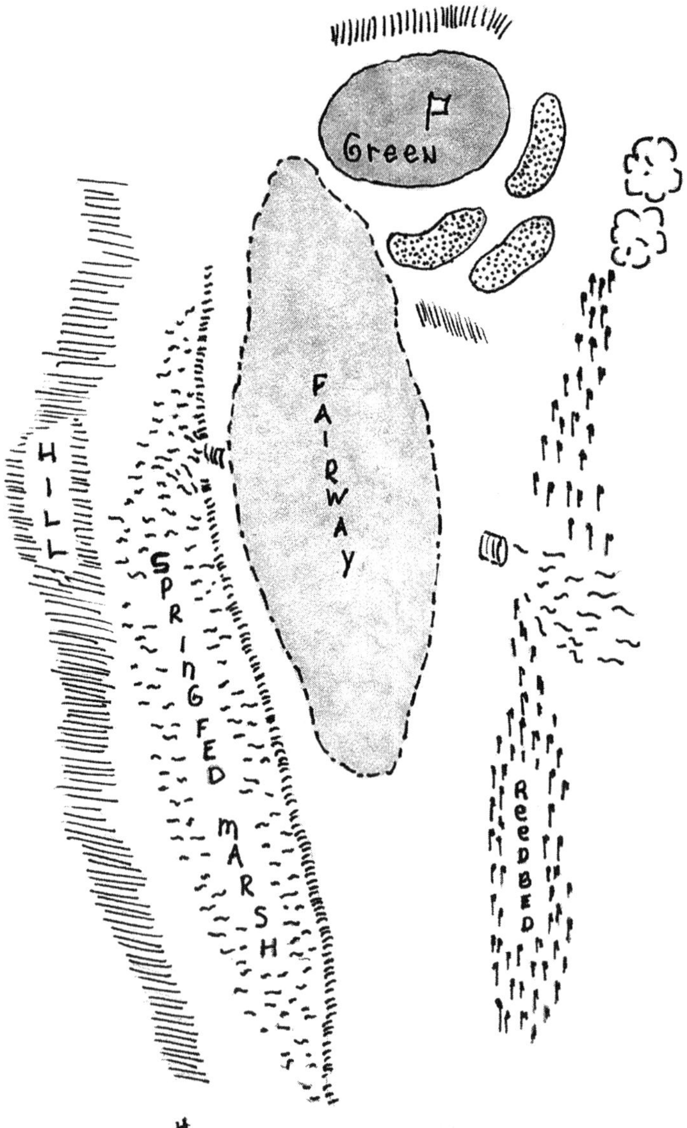
Green
FAIRWAY
HILL
SPRING FED MARSH
REED BED
TEE
Hole #7

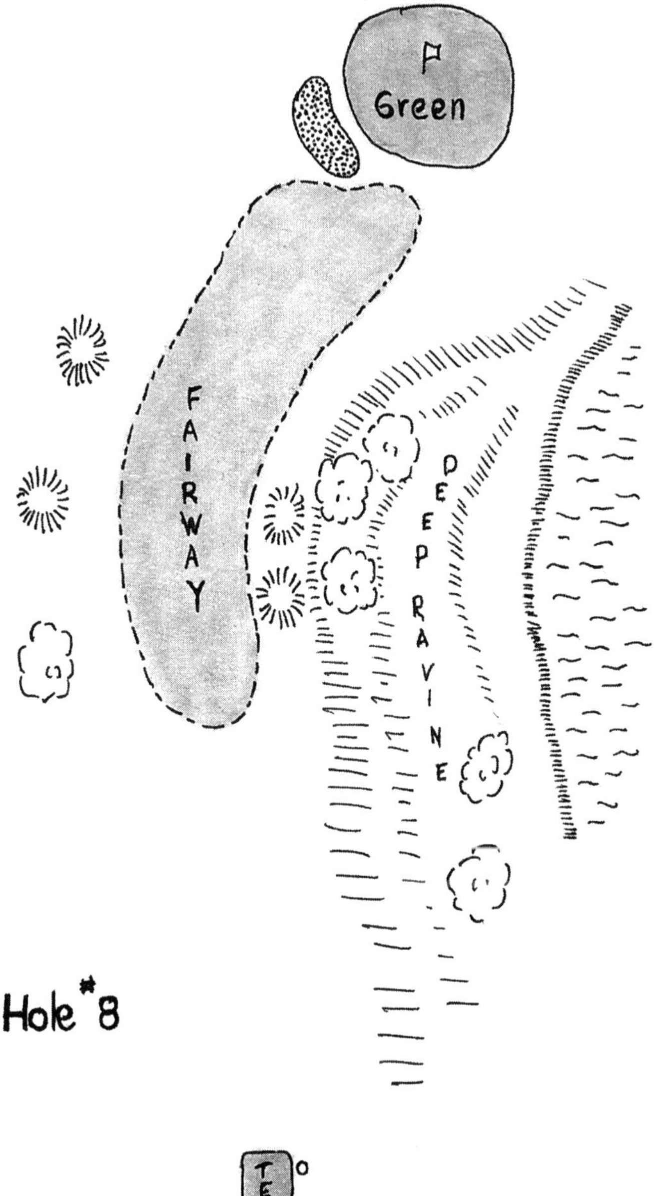
Green
FAIRWAY
DEEP RAVINE
Hole #8
TEE